Ships and Boats

Written by
Jill Atkins

Ransom

There are lots of kinds of ships and boats out at sea, on rivers and on lakes.

Ships are bigger than boats.

As a ship travels fast through the water, it will make a wash behind it. This is called the ship's wake.

Is this the longest of all the ships?
It is a container ship.

Can you see all the containers on the ship?

What do you think might be inside the containers?

Where is the ship going?

Container ships deliver cargo to distant lands. The trip will take a long time, so the crew take turns to keep a look out.

This is an oil tanker. Its hold is full of oil.

Sometimes tankers are full of gas,
petrol or coal.

Some ships travel near the North or South Pole, where it is freezing cold.

These ships are strong so they can cut through the frozen water.

This kind of ship takes people on holiday.

The people sleep in a cabin and
eat their meals on the ship.

There is a pool on the ship too, for people to swim in.

Long ago, ships looked like this.

They are called sailing ships. They used the wind in their sails to help them travel through the water.

This ship uses its sails, too.
It is called a junk.

Boats are not as big as ships.

Some boats are for fun, but some are useful and helpful.

The members of the crew of a lifeboat are so brave. They often go out to sea in a storm.

They will attempt to save lives if a boat or ship is sinking.

The crew of this fishing boat will spend a long time at sea. They need to get lots of fish to sell at the market.

Sometimes they go through a storm. If the storm is bad, the crew might get sea-sick.

They may need the lifeboat as well!

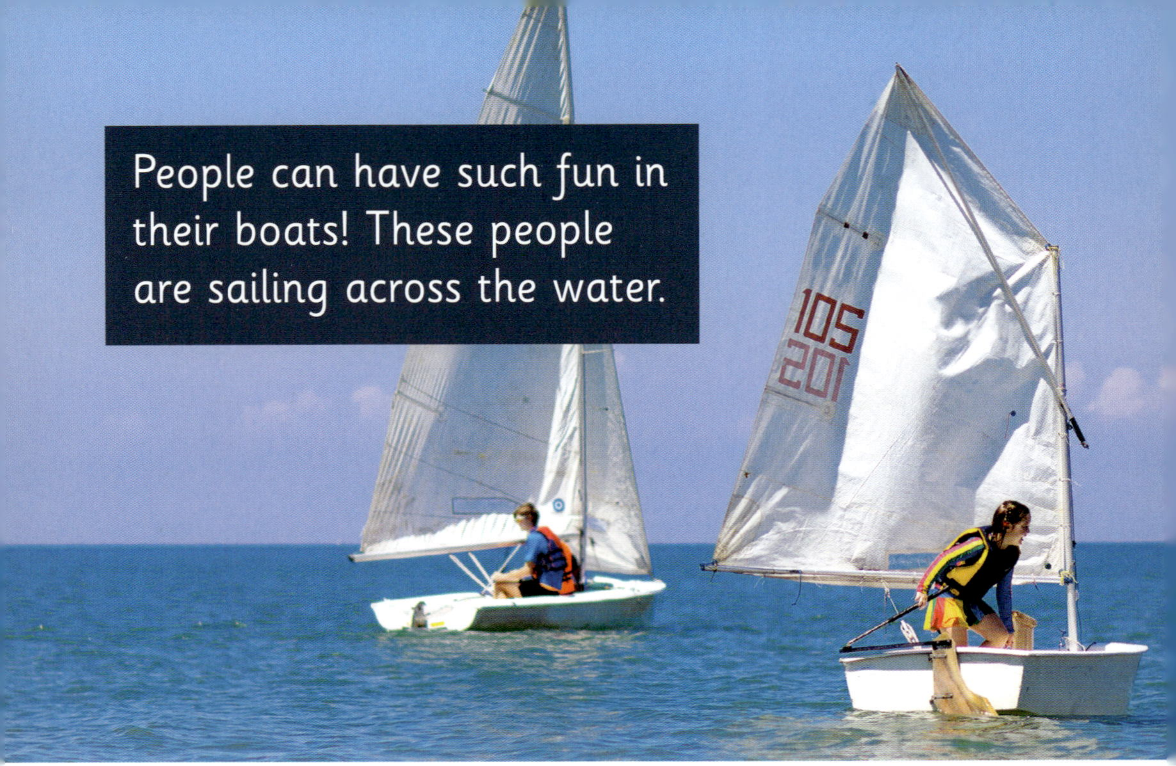

People can have such fun in their boats! These people are sailing across the water.

These men are fishing from their boat.

These people are speeding through the waves. The boat is fast.

One of these boats will get to the winning post first. They do not want to be last!

These people are white-water rafting! They must hang on as their boat travels down the rapids!

Do you want to have a go at that?